COMETS

KATE RIGGS

Creative Education • Creative Paperbacks

Published by Creative Education and Creative Paperbacks
P.O. Box 227, Mankato, Minnesota 56002
Creative Education and Creative Paperbacks are imprints of The Creative Company
www.thecreativecompany.us

Design and production by Chelsey Luther
Printed in the United States of America

Photographs by Corbis (Alan Dyer, Inc/Visuals Unlimited, Alex Cherney/Science
Photo Library, Mark Garlick/Science Photo Library, Tony Hallas/Science Faction,
Detlev van Ravenswaay/Science Photo Library, Roger Ressmeyer, Monsignor
Ronald Royer/Science Photo Library), deviantART (AlmightyHighElf), Dreamstime
(Mack2happy, Oriontrail), Getty Images (Getty Images, Kauko Helavuo), NASA
(NASA/ESA/Hubble SM4 ERO Team, NASA/JPL-Caltech/STScI), Science Source
(Mark Garlick), Shutterstock (Georgios Kollidas, Ohmega1982, solarseven),
SuperStock (Exactostock), Wikipedia (E. Kolmhofer, H. Raab; Johannes-Kepler-
Observatory, Linz, Austria)

Library of Congress Cataloging-in-Publication Data
Riggs, Kate.
Comets / Kate Riggs.
p. cm. — (Across the universe)
Summary: A young scientist's guide to orbiting comets, including how they interact
with other elements in the universe and emphasizing how questions
and observations can lead to discovery.
Includes index.
ISBN 978-1-60818-481-1 (hardcover)
ISBN 978-1-62832-081-7 (pbk)
1. Comets—Juvenile literature. I. Title.
QB721.5.R54 2015
523.6—dc23   2014002082

CCSS: RI.1.1, 2, 3, 4, 5, 6, 7; RI.2.1, 2, 3, 5, 6, 7, 10; RI.3.1, 3, 5, 7, 8; RF.2.3, 4; RF.3.3

First Edition
9 8 7 6 5 4 3 2 1

Pages 20–21 "Astronomy at Home"
activity instructions adapted from
the Center for Science Education
at UC Berkeley:
http://cse.ssl.berkeley.edu
/AtHomeAstronomy/activity_05.html

TABLE OF CONTENTS

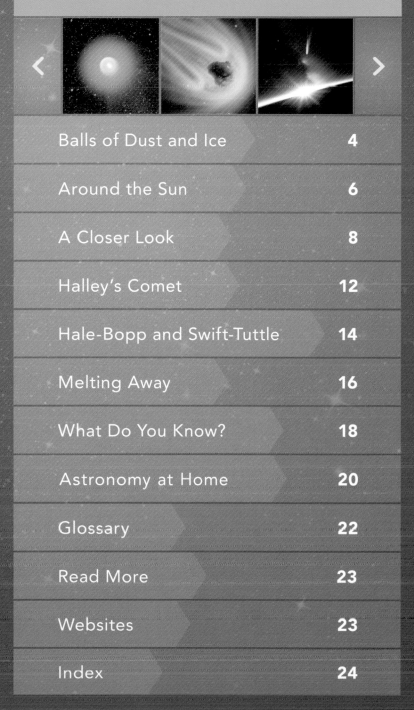

Did you know that comets are balls of ice and dust that come from outer space? Scientists called astronomers study comets. Many comets **orbit** the sun near the **planet** Neptune. The sun's heat and wind make gas and dust trail from a comet. These are called tails.

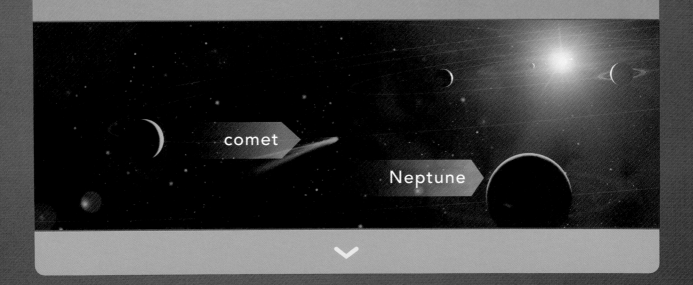

comet

Neptune

Comets are sometimes called "dirty snowballs."

comet tail

Sometimes **gravity** pushes a comet closer to the sun. These comets go around the sun faster than ones that are farther away. There are two kinds of comets. Short-period comets take less than 200 years to orbit the sun. Long-period comets take as long as 30 million years!

Solar System

Comet Hale-Bopp
2,300–2,500 years

Halley's Comet
76 years

Comet Wild (*VILT*) 2 is a short-period comet.

Astronomers have studied comets for hundreds of years. Comets that pass close to Earth can be seen at night. They are best viewed through **telescopes**. Spacecraft can take close-up pictures of comets. Then astronomers can see things like the comet's **nucleus**.

Telescope at Mauna Kea, Hawaii, USA

The Deep Space 1 spacecraft took pictures of Comet Borrelly's nucleus in 2001.

When a comet is closest
to the sun, it is at a point
called perihelion.

HALLEY'S COMET

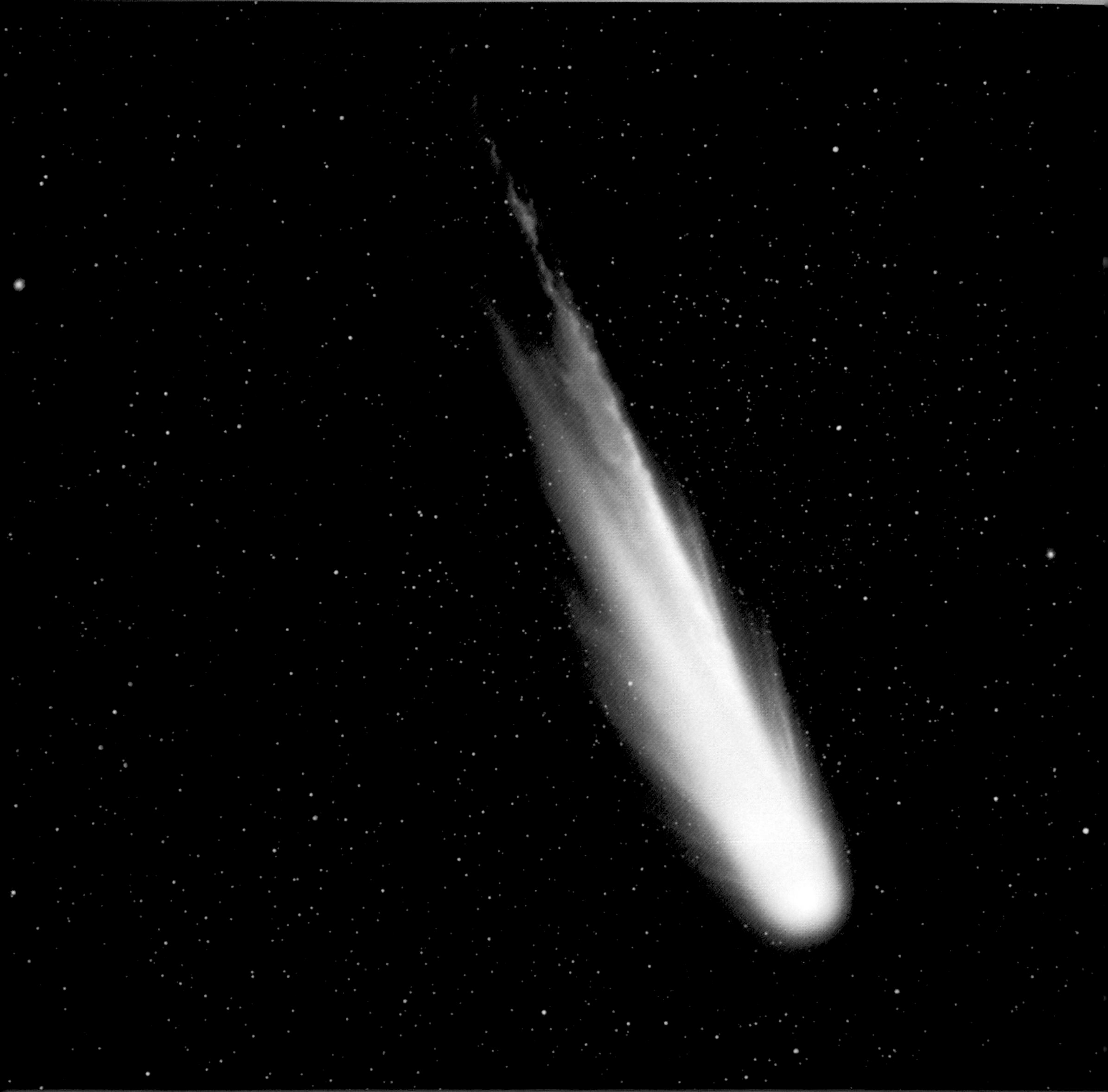

The most famous short-period comet is Halley's Comet. It is 55 million miles (89 million km) from the sun. It can be seen every 75 or 76 years. In 1986, five spacecraft studied Halley's Comet in detail.

Halley's Comet was named after English astronomer Edmond Halley.

Comet Hale-Bopp appeared in 1996 and 1997. It was the largest and brightest comet ever seen. It will not come back again until the year 4380! Every August, we can see **meteors**, thanks to another comet. Comet Swift-Tuttle gives off a cloud of dust. Meteoroids from that dust burn up in our **atmosphere** as meteors.

comet

meteoroids

atmosphere

meteors

Meteoroids in the Perseids meteor shower hit the atmosphere at 132,000 miles (212,433 km) per hour.

The longer comets stay in the solar system, the smaller they get. It takes comets thousands (or maybe even millions) of years to melt away.

Comet Hyakutake was found in 1996 and will not return for 14,000 years!

Tell someone what you know about comets! What else can you discover?

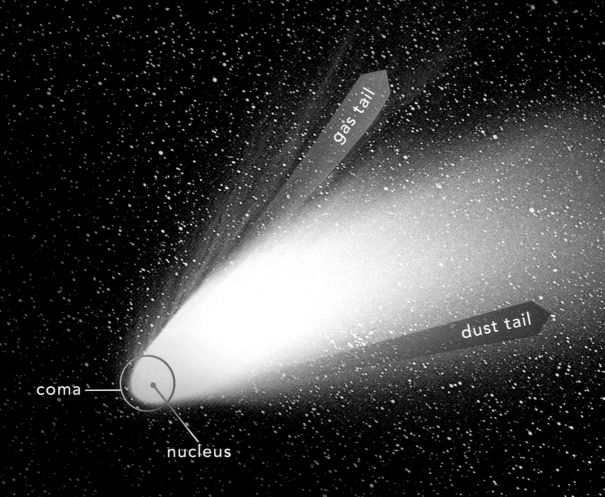

gas tail

dust tail

coma

nucleus

nucleus

MAKE METEOR CRATERS

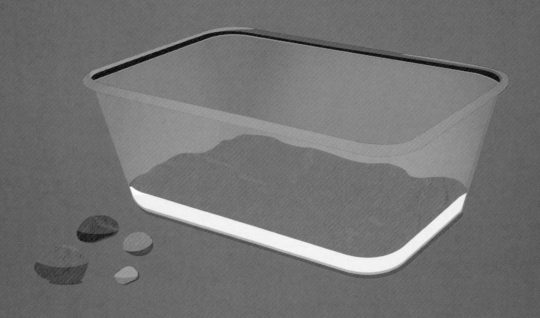

What you need

A shallow box or pan filled with flour about an inch deep, instant cocoa sprinkled on top of the flour, small rocks of various sizes

What you do

Starting with the smallest pebble, drop each rock into the pan. Do smaller rocks make smaller craters? Try throwing the rocks from different heights and angles. What happens to the shape made in the flour each time?

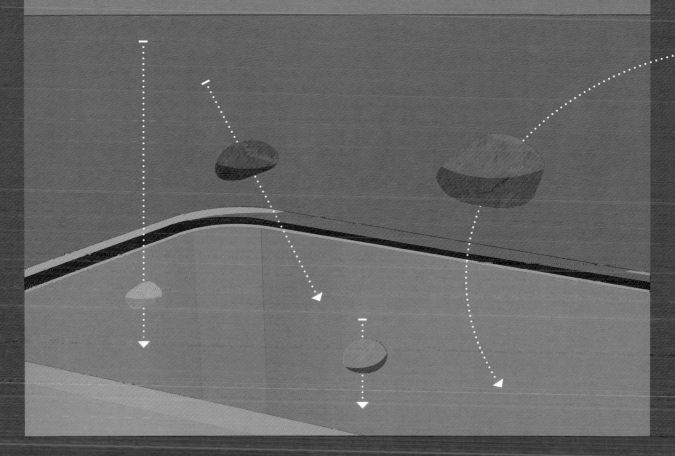

atmosphere   the gases, or air, surrounding Earth

gravity   the force that pulls objects toward each other

meteors   chunks of stone or metal that heat up and glow as they pass through Earth's atmosphere; also called shooting stars

nucleus   the center, or core, of something

orbit   the path a planet, moon, or other object takes around something else in outer space

planet   a rounded object that moves around a star

telescopes   viewing tools that make objects that are far away appear closer

READ MORE

Simon, Seymour. *Comets, Meteors, and Asteroids.* New York: HarperCollins, 1998.

Zobel, Derek. *The Hubble Telescope.* Minneapolis: Bellwether Media, 2010.

WEBSITES

Astronomy Games for Kids
http://www.kidsastronomy.com/fun/index.htm
Play games and learn more about comets and astronomy.

Quiz Your Noodle: Comets and Meteors
http://kids.nationalgeographic.com/kids/games/puzzlesquizzes/quizyournoodle-comets-and-meteors/
Test what you know about comets and meteors!

INDEX